Moving t [barcode: CW00802548]

Mai ĸ

A Study Guide to the Second Gospel

By Michael Penny

ISBN: 978-1-78364-538-1

www.obt.org.uk

****

THE OPEN BIBLE TRUST
Fordland Mount, Upper Basildon,
Reading, RG8 8LU, UK

Introducing Mark

I never approach Mark's Gospel without excitement. Here we have one of the earliest documents of the New Testament, it being written before either Matthew or Luke. Some commentators feel it may have been written even before Paul's first letter, that to the Galatians, which he wrote from Antioch at the end of Acts 14 (verses 26-28). This was after Paul's first missionary journey but before the Jerusalem Council.

John Mark was from Jerusalem and his mother was close to Peter (Acts 12:12). Barnabas was his cousin (Colossians 4:10) and he left Jerusalem and went with Paul and Barnabas to Antioch is Syria. He then accompanied them on their first journey. They left Antioch in Syria and sailed from Seleucia to Salamis on Cyprus (Acts 13:5-6). There Barnabas, and presumably Mark, had many relatives (Acts 4:36). They travelled through the whole Island to Paphos and then boarded a ship bound for Perga and Pamphylia. Their plan was to travel inland into Galatia but for some reason, some *not-too-good* reason one presumes from Acts 15:37-38, Mark left them and returned to Jerusalem (Acts 13:13).

What was it that caused Mark to leave Barnabas and Paul in their exciting adventures? Was he not up to the pressure? Was it lack of maturity? Was it fear of the unknown as, up until then, he had been close to relatives on Cyprus? Was it a crisis of faith? We may never know, but we do know that he went back to Jerusalem and there, I am sure, he did a lot of thinking - and probably a lot of talking also, to people like Peter. Clearly Peter had deep affection for Mark and refers to him as "my son" (1 Peter 5;13).

Some people have called Mark's Gospel, *Peter's* Gospel. It has been suggested that it contains incidents in the life of our Lord Jesus Christ which Peter recalled and either related, dictated, or discussed with Mark. I prefer the last of these suggestions. If Mark was lacking in Christian maturity or did have a crisis in his faith, who better to talk to than Peter?

While Mark was in Jerusalem talking to Peter and, possibly, compiling the document we call Mark's Gospel, Paul and Barnabas travelled through Galatia and back to Antioch in Syria. Then Paul had troubling news from Galatia; certain Christian Jews were teaching that Gentiles had to be circumcised to be saved. Paul wrote his Galatian epistle to deal with the problem. He could not go there himself because similar problems had arisen in Antioch (Acts 15:1). To clarify this issue of Gentile circumcision, Paul and Barnabas were sent to Jerusalem to discuss the matter with Peter and James and the other apostles. They agreed that Gentile Christians need neither be circumcised nor keep the Law of Moses, and a letter to that effect was written. Paul and Barnabas, and others including John Mark, took that letter to Antioch (Acts 15:27,37).

After a while Paul and Barnabas decided that they would like to return and revisit the Christians on Cyrpus and in Galatia, those whom they had seen some years earlier. Barnabas wanted to take John Mark, but Paul refused as Mark "had deserted them in Pamphylia and had not continued with them in the work" (Acts 15:38). They could not agree and so Barnabas took Mark and sailed to Cyprus, while Paul took Silas and travelled to Syria and Cilicia, on through Tarsus, back to Galatia, into Asia and then into Europe.

However strong may have been Paul's disapproval of Mark, it was not to be long-lasting. In Colossians 4:10 we read that Mark was there with Paul, tending his needs when Paul was under house arrest in Rome. And then later, when Paul was rearrested and re-imprisoned in a much more hostile environment, he asked Timothy to "Get Mark and bring him with you, because he is helpful to me in my ministry" (2 Timothy 4:11). What was it that changed Paul's mind about Mark? Did Mark's Gospel have a part to play in this?

When writing to the Corinthians Paul stated that, "Christ died for our sins *according to the Scriptures*, that he was buried, that he was raised on the third day *according to the Scriptures*" (1 Corinthians 15:3-4). To what Scriptures was Paul referring? Something in our Old Testament? If so, what is the chapter and verse? Could it be some New Testament writings? The Gospel of Mark perhaps?

Certainly Peter viewed some of Paul's writing as *Scripture* (2 Peter 3:16), and Paul may well have viewed the Gospel of Mark as *Scripture*. He wrote to the Corinthians during his two year stay in Ephesus (Acts 19:10), thus if Mark had written his gospel when I have suggested here, several years had passed. By this time it may have been copied a number of times, and was probably well-known.

771 Questions on Mark

These questions first appeared in a series published in *Search* magazine, and they were so well received that it has been decided to publish them so that other may benefit from them.

However, it is suggested that readers do not attempt to answer all questions on a particular chapter at one time. The questions on a chapter may be sufficient for two or three sessions of private study or house fellowship discussions.

We suggest the reader may like to:

- First read right through the Gospel of Mark.
- Then to read the whole of the particular chapter being studied.
- Then to read the section on which a group of questions is based.

This will give the reader the context of the questions.

Questions on Mark Chapter 1

Mark 1:1-8; John the Baptist prepares the way

1. What does the word 'gospel' mean?
2. Which chapter and verse in Isaiah open Mark's Gospel?
3. In Isaiah read the two verses either side of the one Mark quoted. What do they mean?
4. Where was John baptising people?
5. Was there sufficient water to totally immerse the people who wished to be baptised?
6. Do we know the manner in which John did baptise?
7. What was John preaching?
8. How deep was the River Jordan in this desert region, east of Jericho and just north of the Dead Sea?
9. What did John wear?
10. Was there any significance in what John wore? If so, what?
11. What did John eat?
12. Was there any significance in what John ate? If so, what?
13. To whom was John referring when he spoke of One who would come *after* him?
14. What two things did John say about this One Who was to come?

Mark 1:9-13; The baptism and temptation of Jesus

15. How far is it from Nazareth to the Jordan, near Jericho?
16. What route would the Lord Jesus have followed?
17. How long would the journey have taken?
18. What two things happened after Christ's baptism?
19. What three things did the voice from heaven say about the Lord?
20. Where did Christ go after His baptism?
21. Why did He go there?

22. What happened to Him there?
23. Why did angels attend Him?

Mark 1:14-20; The calling of the first disciples

24. Why was John put in prison?
25. Where did Jesus go?
26. What is the difference between "gospel" (v 1) and "good news" (v 14)?
27. What "good news" did the Lord Jesus proclaim?
28. In what ways, if any, did Christ's message differ from that of John's? (Cp. Matthew 3:2 and Matthew 4:17.)
29. Was this the first time Christ had seen Simon and his brother Andrew? Or does Mark's Gospel not contain anything on the earlier ministry of the Lord Jesus which is found in the other gospels?
30. Who were the next two disciples to be called?

Mark 1:21-28; Jesus drives out an evil spirit

31. Where is Capernaum?
32. Where did Jesus and His disciples go in Capernaum?
33. Why did they go there?
34. Why were the people amazed at Christ's teaching?
35. Why did the evil spirit say what it said?
36. How did the evil spirit know who Jesus was?
37. How did the Lord answer the evil spirit?
38. What did He do to the evil spirit?
39. What was the people's reaction to this incident?
40. Did the people keep this incident a secret?

Mark 1:29-34; Jesus heals many

41. Where did the Lord and the disciples go once they left the synagogue?
42. What did they find there?
43. What did Jesus do about it?
44. What happened that evening?
45. Why didn't the Lord Jesus allow the demons to say Who He was?

Mark 1:35-39; Jesus prays in a solitary place

46. Why did Jesus go to a solitary place to pray?
47. Why did the disciples go to look for Him?
48. What did they tell him?
49. What did the Lord tell them?
50. Where did they go?

Mark 1:40-45; A man with leprosy

51. Why didn't Jesus want the man cured of leprosy to tell anyone?
52. Does this mean Jesus never wanted the man to tell anyone, or that he didn't want him to tell anyone until *after* he had been to the priest?
53. Why did the Lord Jesus tell the man to show himself to the priest, and to offer certain sacrifices?
54. What was the purpose of these sacrifices?
55. Was the Lord Jesus undermining or supporting the Mosaic Law?
56. What did the man actually do?
57. What was the result of the man's disobedience?

Questions on Mark Chapter 2

Mark 2:1-12; Jesus heals a paralytic

58. How many people gathered at the synagogue in Capernaum?

59. What did Jesus do there?

60. What did some men do with a paralytic?

61. What did the Lord say to the paralytic?

62. Were the teachers of the law correct in saying, "Who can forgive sins but God alone?"

63. Were the teachers of the law correct in accusing Jesus of blasphemy? If so, why? If not, why not?

64. Which is easier? To *say*, "Your sins are forgiven?" or to *say*, "Get up, take your mat and walk"?

65. How did this miracle show that Christ had the authority to forgive sins? (Cp. Isaiah 35:3-6.)

66. How did this miracle show that Jesus was the Son of Man (2:10) and the Son of God (1:1)?

67. What did Jesus say to the paralytic?

68. What happened?

69. What effect did this have on the people watching?

Mark 2:13-17; The calling of Levi

70. What was Levi's other name?

71. What was Levi's work?

72. Where did Jesus have dinner?

73. Who ate with Him?

74. What question did the Pharisees ask the disciples?

75. Why did they ask this question?

76. What answer did Jesus give them?

77. What did the answer mean?

Mark 2: 18-22; Jesus questioned about fasting

78. How often did John's disciples fast?

79. How often did the Pharisees fast?

80. How often did the Law saw the Jews should fast?

81. How often did Christ's disciples fast?

82. Who is the bridegroom?

83. Who are the guests?

84. Why cannot the guests fast when the bridegroom is with them?

85. When was the bridegroom taken away?

86. Did the guests fast that day?

87. What is the meaning and point of the parable about not sewing a patch of unshrunk cloth on to an old garment?

88. What is the meaning and point of the parable about not putting new wine into old   wineskins?

Mark 2:23-28; Lord of the Sabbath

89. Were the disciples doing anything that broke the Law of Moses?

90. Were the disciples doing anything that broke the Pharisaic additions to the Law?

91. What incident in the life of David did Christ refer to?

92. Why did He refer to this incident as it had nothing to do with the Sabbath?

93. What did he mean when He said, "The Sabbath was made for man, not man for the Sabbath"?

94. What did He mean when He said, "The Son of Man is Lord even of the Sabbath"?

95. Did the Lord Jesus Christ ever break the Sabbath Law?

96. Did He ever break the Pharisaic additions to that Law?

Questions on
Mark Chapter 3

Mark 3:1-6; Lord of the Sabbath

97. Why were some wanting to accuse Jesus?

98. What were they wanting to accuse Him of?

99. Why did those who wanted to accuse Jesus think it was wrong to heal on the Sabbath?

100. Does the Law of Moses saying anything about healing on the Sabbath?

101. What questions did the Lord ask those who wanted to accuse Him?

102. What was their answer?

103. Why did the Lord look at them in anger?

104. Why was He deeply distressed?

105. After he had healed the man, what did the Pharisees do?

106. Who were the Pharisees?

107. Who were the Herodians?

108. Why did they want to kill Jesus?

Mark 3:7-12; Crowds follows Jesus

109. To which lake did Jesus withdraw?

110. Where was Idumea?

111. What is meant by "the regions across the Jordan"?

112. How far was it from the lake to (a) Tyre, (b) Sidon?

113. How long would it have taken these people to have travelled from (a) Tyre, (b) Sidon?

114. Why did people from all these places want to come and see Jesus?

115. What did the evil spirits call Jesus?

116. Why did He give them strict orders not to tell people Who he was?

Mark 3:13-19; Appointing the Twelve

117. Which hills did Jesus go up into?

118. What does the word "apostle" mean?

119. Why did he chose twelve?

120. For what were the *three* purposes were they appointed?

121. Why did the Lord give Simon the name "Peter"?

122. What are the meanings of the names "Simon" and "Peter"?

123. Why did the Lord give James and John the name "Boanerges?

124. What is the meaning of "Boanerges"?

125. Why did the Lord chose Judas Iscariot?

Mark 3:20-30; Beelzebub

126. Why did the crowd gather at the house?

127. Who is meant by Jesus' *family*?

128. Why did His family say, "He is out of his mind?"

129. What did they mean by it?

130. Who were "the teachers of the law"?

131. Who is meant by "Beelzebub?"

132. Where is Beelzebub referred to in the Law of Moses or in the Old Testament?

133. What was taught about Beelzebub in New Testament times?

134. What does the parable mean?

135. What is the main point of this parable? (For a full treatment of this see *40 Problem Passages* by Michael Penny; problem passages 10 deals with "The unforgivable sin.")

136. The teachers of the law of Jesus that, "He is possessed by Beelzebub! By the prince of demons he is driving out demons." How did this blaspheme the Holy Spirit?

137. Is it possible to "blaspheme the Holy Spirit" in this way in this dispensation?

138. Why did the Lord speak this parable?

Mark 3:31-35; The Lord's family

139. Which members of the Lord's family arrived?
140. What other members of his family were there?
141. Why didn't they go into the house?
142. What did the Lord say when he was told, "Your mother and brothers are outside looking for you?"
143. Why did He say that?
144. What did He mean by it?

Questions on Mark Chapter 4

Mark 4:1-8; The Parable of the Sower

145. What is a parable?
146. What happened to the seed which fell (a) on the path, (b) on the rocky places, (c) amongst the thorns, (d) on the good soil?
147. What was the normal return from a harvest at that time?

Mark 4:9-13; Understanding Parables

148. Why did the Lord say, "He who has ears to ear, let him ear?"
149. What does that expression mean?
150. Some people think the Lord Jesus used parables to make things clearer. If that is the case, (a) why did He say, "He who has ears to ear, let him ear"?
(b) why did the apostle ask him about parables?
(c) why did He say, "The secret of the kingdom of God has been given to you. But to those on the outside everything is said in parables"? (First you may need to discuss and define the kingdom of God.)
151. What three reasons did the Lord give for speaking to those on the outside in parables?
152. Do those reasons imply that the Lord spoke in parables to make things clearer, or to veil the meaning of what He was teaching?
153. Did the disciples under stand the parable of the sower before the Lord gave His interpretation?
154. Would we understand the parable of the sower if we had not been given the interpretation?

Mark 4:14-20; The interpretation of the sower

155. What is the interpretation of (a) the seed along the path, (b) the birds?

156. What is the interpretation of (a) the seed along the rocky places, (b) the shallow soil, (c) the sun?

157. What is the interpretation of (a) the seed among thorns, (b) the thorns?

158. What is the interpretation of (a) the good soil, (b) the crop, (c) the thirty, sixty or even a hundred times what is sown?

159. Often, in parables, there is one main point which usually comes towards the end, and whose force is brought home by an extreme exaggeration, or an hyperbole. Why was producing a crop of "thirty, sixty, or even a hundred times what was sown" an extreme exaggeration to the people on New Testament times?

Mark 4:21-23; A lamp on a stand

160. To what things is the Lord referring to who He spoke of (a) "whatever is hidden", (b) "whatever is disclosed"?

161. Is He continuing with His teaching on parables? That is, that they hide and conceal teaching about the secret of the kingdom of God, and need to be disclosed and made open? If not, to what is He referring?

162. Why does the Lord, again, use the expression, "If anyone has ears to hear, let him ear?"

163. What does this expression mean? Why did the Lord use it?

Mark 4:24-25; Three sayings

164. Why does the Lord say, "Consider carefully what you hear?" Is He telling people to consider carefully the words of parables? Or is it just general good advice about everything people hear?

165. How do the words, "With the measure you use, it will be measured to you - and even more," follow on from "Consider carefully what you hear"?

166. What did the Lord mean by the words, "With the measure you use, it will be measured to you - and even more"?

167. How do the words, "Whoever has will be given more; whoever does not have, even what he has will be taken from him" follow on from the previous words?

168. What did the Lord mean by the words, "Whoever has will be given more; whoever does not have, even what he has will be taken from him"?

169. Are the words of verse 25 referring to (a) wealth, (b) health, (c) possessions, (d) knowledge, (e) other things? (Compare Matthew 13:10-13)

170. In the light of Matthew 13:10-17, should our understanding of Mark 4:21-25 be strictly limited to the understanding of parables? If so, you may need to revisit some of the above questions; e.g. numbers 160-169.

Mark 4:26-29; The growing seed

171. Who is the "man" in this parable? (Careful! It cannot be the Lord for it says the man does not know how the seed sprouts and grows.)

172. How are verses 26b-29 like the kingdom of God? (First you may need to discuss and define the kingdom of God.)

173. Is there any significance in the term "the harvest"?

Mark 4:30-32; The mustard seed

174. How is the growth of mustard plant like the kingdom of God?

175. Is there any significance in (a) the seed being the smallest, (b) the plant being largest, (c) that birds perch in its shade?

Mark 4:33-34; Understanding Parables

176. Again, does verse 33 imply parables make our Lord's teachings easier or that they were harder to understand?

177. Does the second part of verse 34 imply that parables are easy to understand or that they need to be explained?

178. In the light of your answers to questions 176 and 177, you may need to revisit questions 171-175 on the parables of the Growing Seed and the Mustard Seed.

Mark 4:35-41; The storm

179. Where did the Lord mean by "the other side"?

180. Why did the Lord "rebuke the storm"?

181. How can you rebuke something that is inanimate, that is a-moral?

182. Do the Lord's words to the disciples seem a little harsh? After all, wasn't it natural for them to be afraid? How were they to know He could control the weather?

183. Why were the disciples "terrified"?

184. If what or of whom were they terrified?

Questions on
Mark Chapter 5

Mark 5:1-20; The healing of the demon-possessed man

185. Which lake were they on?

186. Where is "the region of the Gerasenes"?

187. Why is this also called the region of the "Gaderenes"?

188. How could the evil spirit give the man so much strength?

189. If he broke the metals chains on his hands and his feet, when doing this why didn't he break the bones in his arms and his legs?

190. Why did the man cut himself?

191. Was this the evil spirit causing the man to cut himself - and if so, why - or was the man inflicting pain on himself - and if so, why?

192. How did the evil spirit know that Jesus was the "Son of the Most High God?"

193. The Lord Jesus said, "Come out of this man, you evil spirit!" Why did this cause the evil spirit to say, "Swear to God that you won't torture me!"?

194. For what reason did the evil spirit think he might be tortured?

195. Did the evil deserved to be tortured after the way he had tortured the man?

196. In what way did the evil spirit think he might be tortured?

197. Is there any record in the Scriptures of the Lord torturing evil spirits?

> If not, why was the spirit concerned that Christ may torture him?
>
> If there is, where and in what way were they tortured, and for what reason?

198. What did the evil spirit mean by "we are many"? (Cp. Luke 8:26-39)

199. Was there one chief evil spirit who was in command, as a centurion is in charge of a hundred soldiers?

200. Why did the evil spirit not want them (the evil spirit and the demons) to be sent out of the area?

201. Luke 8:31 records that they did not want to get sent into the abyss! What does the Bible say about the abyss?

202. Why were there pigs in the area? After all, it was forbidden in the Law of Moses for Jews to eat pigs!

203. Why did the "demons" ask to go into the pigs?

203. Was there a difference between "the evil spirit" and "the demons"?

204. Why were there such a large herd of pigs in this area? After all, it was forbidden in the Law of Moses for Jews to eat pigs!

205. As there were 2,000 pigs, does that mean that the man was possessed by 2,000 or more demons?

206. What happened to the demons when the pigs died?

207. Why were the people of that area "afraid" when they saw the man sitting there, dressed, and in his right mind?

208. Why did these people ask Jesus to leave their region?

209. Why did the man want to go with the Lord Jesus?

210. Why didn't Christ let the man go with Him?

211. Where was Decapolis?

212. Did demon possession occur in the Old Testament?

213. Did demon possession occur during the Acts period?

214. Did demon possession occur in the books written after Acts?

215. Was demon possession a phenomenon which occurred primarily when Christ was on earth?

216. If so, what was its purpose?

217. Do you understand demon possession as it occurs in the Bible?

218. Does demon possession occur today?

Mark 5:21-43: A dead girl and a sick woman

219. Which lake were they on?

220. Which side of the lake was Christ now on?

221. How did Jairus know that the Lord Jesus had the power to heal?

222. Why did the woman think that if "she" just touched Jesus, rather than He touching her, she would be healed?

223. What happened when she touched His cloak?

224. How did she know she was healed?

225. How did the Lord know that someone had touched Him?

226. How did He know that power had gone out of Him?

227. What is meant by "power"? What "power" was Mark referring to?

228. As there were a big crowd around the Lord, and as many other people must have touched Him, why didn't any of those people take power from the Lord?

229. Why did the woman own up?

230. Why did she tremble with fear?

231. What news came from Jairus' house?

232. What did Jesus want Jairus to believe? (A) That his daughter was still ill, but had not died? (B) That Christ could heal her? (C) That Christ could raise her from the dead? {Note: would Jairus have known, at this point in time, that the Lord Jesus had the power to raise the dead? Had the Lord raised anyone from the dead at this time; either in that area or elsewhere?}

233. Why didn't the Lord let anyone follow Him, expect Peter, James and John?

234. Why did the people at Jairus' house laugh at the Lord Jesus?

235. Why did the Lord put everyone out of the house, except Peter, James and John, and the girl's parents?

236. What did the Lord Jesus do to the girl and what happened?

237. Why did the Lord Jesus give strict orders for the parents (and Peter, James and John) not to tell anyone about this?

238. In spite of His strict orders, everyone who was outside of Jairus' house knew that the girl was dead. Sooner or later they

would see her and know that Jesus had raised her from the dead. In that case, why didn't Christ want them to know at that time?

Questions on Mark Chapter 6

Mark 6:1-6a: A prophet without honour

239. Why were the people in Nazareth, Jesus' home town, amazed by what He taught?

240. What did He teach there? (See Luke 4:14-30.)

241. How man questions did the people raise?

242. What were the names of Jesus' (half-)brothers?

243. How many (half-) sisters did He have?

244. Why did they take offence at Him, after all He had performed miracles?

245. Was the offence in what He taught? If so, what did He teach? (See Luke 4.)

246. How extreme was the offence they took? (See Luke 4.)

247. What does it mean to be "without honour"?

248. Why was it true that a prophet was "without honour" in his home town?

249. Is it true today, that very able people do not receive full recognition is their home towns?

250. Why was it that the Lord Jesus "*could* not do any miracles" in Nazareth?

251. Does it really mean "could" not, or does it mean He "chose" not to do any miracles?

252. What amazed the Lord Jesus Christ?

253. How could the Lord Jesus Christ, Who knew what is in people, be amazed by something?

Mark 6:6b-13: Jesus sends out the Twelve

254. Why did the Lord Jesus send out the Twelve "two by two"? (See Matthew 18:16.)

255. What power did He give them?

256. Why were they to take nothing for the journey?

257. Why were they allowed to take a staff?

258. Why were they to take (a) no bread? (b) No bag? (c) No money? (d) No extra tunic?

259. Why were they allowed to wear sandals?

260. Are these rules applicable to today? Were they applicable during the time covered by the Acts of the Apostles? (See Luke 22:35-36.)

261. Why were they to reside in the same house throughout their stay in any town?

262. For what reason(s) were they to shake the dust off their feet?

263. Why was shaking the dust off their feet a testimony against a town? What did "shaking dust off the feet" symbolise?

264. What did they preach? (See also Matthew 10:1-42.)

265. As it was *not* necessary for sick people to be anointed with oil in order to be healed, why did the Twelve anoint sick people with oil?

Mark 6:14-29: Herod and John the Baptist

266. What had Herod heard about the Lord Jesus?

267. What were the three different opinion people had as to Who was the Lord Jesus?

268. Which one did Herod think to be right? Why did he favour this one?

269. When had Herod arrested John and beheaded him? Was it weeks or months or years before the incident recorded here?

270. Why had Herod arrested John?

271. Why had Herodias nursed a grudge against John?

272. Why was unlawful for a man to marry his brother's wife? Was this against Roman law? Or Jewish Law?

273. Why couldn't Herodias have John put to death?

274. Why did Herod fear John?

275. What was it about John, or what John said, that puzzled Herod?

275. If Herod knew John to be a righteous and holy man, and as he liked to listen to him, why didn't Herod *do* what John taught?

276. Who came to Herod's birthday party?

277. How did Herodias fulfil her grudge and have John killed?

278. Why was Herod distressed?

279. If he was so distressed, why didn't he decline his step-daughter's request?

Mark 6:30-44: Jesus feeds five thousand

280. Why did the Twelve report to the Lord "all they had done and taught"?

281. For what two reasons did the Lord Jesus want to take the Twelve to a quiet place?

282. Where did the Lord and the Twelve travel from and to where were they going? (Cp. Mark 6:1,6,45,53.)

283. How could the people, on foot, get there ahead of the Lord and the Twelve in their boat?

284. Why did the Lord have compassion on the people and start to teach them?

285. How much would it have cost to feed all the people?

286. Did the disciples begrudge spending such a sum on the people?

287. How much food did they actually have?

288. How many people were fed?

289. How much food was left over?

290. How did the Lord increase the food?

291. Does this miracle testify that Jesus was the Christ (Messiah) or the Son of God? (Cp. John 6:1-12 and John 20:30-31.)

Mark 6:45-56: Jesus walks on the water

292. Why did the Lord Jesus send the disciples ahead of Him? (Cp. Mark 6:30-32.)

293. To where did He send the disciples?

294. How could the Lord Jesus walk on water?

295. Why, if He walked out to them, was He about to pass by them?

296. Why were the disciples terrified?

297. Why did they think that He was a ghost?

298. What happened when He climbed into the boat?

299. Why were the disciples amazed?

300. What was it that they did not understand about the loaves? (See question 291.)

301. How were disciples hearts hardened, and why?

302. Did the miracles of walking on the water and calming the storm show that Jesus was the Christ (Messiah) or that He was the Son of God? (Cp. John 6:16-21 and John 20:30-31.)

303. What did the people in Gennesaret do as soon as they saw the Lord Jesus?

304. What did other people do wherever the Lord Jesus went?

305. Did the healing miracles of the Lord Jesus show that He was the Christ (Messiah) or the Son of God? (Cp. John 4:43-54; 5:1-15; 9:1-12 and John 20:30-31.)

Questions on Mark Chapter 7

Mark 7:1-23 Clean and Unclean

306. Why did the Pharisees consider the disciples hands 'unclean'?

307. Were the disciples hands 'unclean' according to the Law of Moses?

308. Is there anything in the Law of Moses about the ceremonial washing of hands for all people?

309. Is there anything in the Law of Moses about the ceremonial washing of anything for anyone? (E.g. see Leviticus 22:2-3; Numbers 8:5.)

310. What other ceremonial washings did the traditions of the elders require?

311. Were any of these commanded by the Law of Moses? If so, which ones?

312. Why didn't the Lord Jesus and His disciples live according to the traditions of the elders?

313. In what way were the Pharisees hypocrites?

314. Why was the worship offered by the Pharisees in vain?

315. What does Christ call the teachings and traditions of the elders?

316. Will 'the traditions of men' always supplant 'the commands of God'?

317. Do the 'traditions' of our church set aside 'the commands of God'?

318. What does it mean to 'nullify' the word of God?

319. In what way did a Corban (a gift devoted to God) nullify the word of God?

320. What other things did the Pharisees teach and allow which nullified the word of God?

321. What traditions are there in our church which nullify the word of God?

322. Why is it that 'what comes out of a man' renders a man unclean?

323. Why is that nothing a person eats, whether it is clean or unclean, can render that person unclean?

324. What does it mean when it states, "Jesus declared all food 'clean'"? **Note:** it cannot mean that the Jews were now allowed to eat such foods as pork, for in Matthew 5:17-19 Christ upholds the Law and states "not the smallest letter, not the least stroke of a pen, will by any means disappear from the Law until everything is accomplished". (For a full treatment of this subject see problem passage 16 in Michael Penny's *40 Problem Passages*.)

325. What things that come out of a man make him unclean?

326. Why do these things make a man unclean?

Mark 7:24-30 The Syrophoencian Woman

327. Why didn't the Lord want people to know He was in that region?

328. What nationality was the woman?

329. Why didn't the Lord immediately respond to her request?

330. When the Lord Jesus refers to 'the children' (v 27), to whom is He referring?

331. When the Lord Jesus refers to 'dogs' (v 27) to whom is he referring?

332. Why was it not right to take the 'children's' bread and toss it to the 'dogs'?

333. What did the woman's reply mean?

334. Why was the Lord Jesus impressed with the woman's reply?

335. Why did her reply prompt the Lord Jesus to grant her request?

Mark 7:31-37 The Deaf and Dumb Man

336. How far a journey would it be from Tyre, through Sidon, passed the Sea of Galilee, and into Decapolis?

337. How long would such a journey take?

338. Why did Christ put His fingers in the man's ears?

339. Why did He spit and touch the man's tongue?

340. Could the Lord have healed the man without touching his ears and tongue?

341. Why did the Lord command the people not to tell anyone?

342. Did the people obey the Lord's command for them not to tell anyone about this miracle?

343. Was it humanly possible for these people to keep quiet about such an event?

Questions on Mark Chapter 8

Mark 8:1-10 Jesus Feeds the Four Thousand

344. Verse one states that "another" large crowd gathered. On what previous occasion, or occasions, did a large crowd gather?

345. How long had this crowd been with Jesus?

346. Why did they have nothing to eat?

347. Why had these people gathered in such a "remote" place?

348. How many basketfuls of bread was left over from the seven loaves?

349. What does this miracle signify about Jesus?

350. Where is the region of Dalmanutha?

Mark 8:11-21 The Yeast of the Pharisees and Herod

351. Why did the Pharisees question Jesus?

352. Why did they want to test Him?

353. Were they right to test him?

354. What would the Pharisees consider a "sign from heave"?

355. What test would Jesus pass if He produced such a sign? What would it prove to the Pharisees?

356. Why did He refuse to give them such a sign?

357. What is the "the yeast of the Pharisees and Herod"? What does "yeast" symbolise in general? What does it symbolise in particular with respect to (a) the Pharisees, (b) Herod?

358. Why didn't the disciples understand this?

359. In what way were the disciple's hearts hardened?

360. How much earlier than feeding the 4,000 did Jesus feed the 5,000?

Mark 8:22-26 The Healing of the Blind Man

361. Where is Bethsaida?

362. As Jesus healed all other people immediately, completely, and instantly, why did He heal this man in two stages?

363. Is there anything symbolic in the healing of the man in two stages?

364. Why did the Lord tell the man not to go into the village?

Mark 8:27-30 Peter's Confession

365. Why did the Lord ask the disciples who other people thought that He was?

366. Why would some say "John the Baptist"? Isn't that a non-sensical answer?

367. What would some say Elijah? Is that non-sensical? (Malachi 3:1; 4:5-6.)

368. Why would some say "one of the prophets"? Did they have some specific Old Testament prophet in mind, or were they saying that He was another prophet *like* Isaiah or Jeremiah?

369. If this question - Who do people say that Jesus is? - were asked today, what sorts of answers would people give?

370. Would some of those answers be non-sensical?

371. Why did the Lord want to know who the disciples thought He was?

372. What was Peter's answers?

373. Why did the Lord warn Peter not to tell anyone? Why did He need to **warn** Peter?

374. If you were asked your opinion, who would you say Jesus is?

375. Should you not tell people this?

Mark 8:31-33 Jesus predicts His death.

376. What four things did the Lord begin to teach the disciples?

377. Was this the first time they had heard such things?

378. Why did Peter rebuke the Lord for teaching these things?

379. Didn't Peter hear the fourth thing the Lord taught?

380. Why did the Lord refer to Peter as "Satan"?

381 In what was did Peter have in minds the things of men?

Mark 8:34-38 Jesus talks to the crowd

382 What three things had a person to do if they wanted to come after Jesus?

383 o these apply to Christian today?

384 What does it mean to "deny himself"?

385 What does it mean to "take up his cross"?

386 What does it mean to want to "save" his life?

387 What does it mean to "lose" his life?

388 How will a person who "saves" his life, "lose" it?

389 What does it mean to "lose" his life for Christ?

390 What does it mean to "lose" his life for the gospel?

391 ow will a person who "loses" his life, "save" it?

392 What does it mean to forfeit a soul?

393 Were some of the followers of Jesus Christ ashamed of Him and His teaching?

394. Are some believers today ashamed of Jesus Christ and His teachings? If so, on what occasions or in what circumstances?

Questions on Mark Chapter 9

Mark 9:1 Not taste death

395. What did the Lord Jesus Christ mean when He said, "Some who are standing here will not taste death before they see the kingdom of God come with power"?

396. Some think this refers to the Transfiguration, but at the Transfiguration, did the kingdom of God come with 'power'?

397. There are other verses which make similar statements; e.g. Matthew 109:23; 16:28; 24:34. What did the Lord Jesus Christ mean in each of these? (For a full answer see Problem Passage number 12 in Michael Penny's *40 Problem Passages*, available from The Open Bible Trust.)

Mark 9:2-13 The Transfiguration

398. Why did the Lord Jesus Christ take only Peter, James and John with Him?

399. What happened at the Transfiguration?

400. Why was it Moses and Elijah who appeared at the Transfiguration, rather than, say, people like David or Isaiah?

401. How did Peter, James and John know that it was Moses and Elijah?

402. Why were the three disciples so frightened?

403. Why did Peter suggest building three shelters?

404. What was the purpose of the shelters?

405. Verse 6 implies Peter was wrong to suggest building three shelters. What was wrong with what Peter said?

406. Had Moses and Elijah been there, or had they seen a vision of them? (See Matthew 17:9 *KJV*.)

407. Why did the Lord order the three not to tell anyone else what they had seen?

408. Why didn't they understand what "rising from the dead" meant? (See Luke 9:45; 18:34.)

409. What does the Old Testament say about Elijah coming first? (See Malachi 3:1; 4:5-6.)

410. To whom was the Lord referring when He said "Elijah has come"?

411. Did that person fulfill the Elijah prophecies? (e.g. was all restored; and see also Malachi 4:5-6.)

412. As the Son of Man was rejected and suffered, were all things restored and the hearts of the people turned to the Lord?

413. If they weren't, does that imply that the Elijah prophecies are unfulfilled and that Elijah is to come to Israel some time in the future, before the Lord's return?

Mark 9:14-29 The Healing of a Boy with an Evil Spirit

414. Who were the "other" disciples?

415. Why were the crowd "overwhelmed with wonder" when they saw the Lord?

416. Were the words "unbelieving generation" a description of the crowd or the other disciples?

417. Was the father confident in his belief that Jesus could cure his son?

418. Why couldn't the disciples drive out this particular demon? (See the footnote on this verse in the *NIV*.)

Mark 9:30-37 Jesus and His Disciples

419. Why did the Lord Jesus want to be away from the crowds?

420. Why didn't the disciples understand the plain words which the Lord spoke? (See Luke 9:45; 18:34.)

421. Why were they "afraid" to ask Him for an explanation?

422. Were the disciples ashamed of what they were arguing about?

423. What must a person do to be first in the Lord's estimation?

424. What does it mean to welcome someone "in Christ's name"?

425. What point was the Lord making when He said that the people must welcome little children in His name?

Mark 9:38-41 Others driving our Demons

426. How many other people were driving out demons?

427. Were these other followers of Christ or not?

428. What does it mean to give a cup of water "in Christ's name"?

429. Why would such a simple thing as giving a cup of water to one of the disciples ensure a person would not lose their reward?

Mark 9:42-50 Causing to sin

430. To what sin, or sins, was the Lord referring when he said "if anyone causes one of these little ... to sin"?

431. What will happen to a person who does cause such a child to sin?

432. Why would it be better for such a person to be thrown into the sea and drown?

433. What happens to the people cast into hell? (See Revelation 20:11-15.)

434. In verses 43-47, is the Lord talking literally or is He using a figure of speech?

435. If a figure of speech, which one?

436. Is verse 48 literal or figurative? (Can a worm live in a fire?)

437. Verse 48 is a quotation from Isaiah 66:24. Is it referring to people who are dead or alive?

438. What does "everyone will be salted with fire" mean? (Is 1 Corinthians 3:11-15 a help?)

439. What does the Lord mean by "have salt in yourselves"?

440. Why does He tell them to "be at peace with each other"?
(See Mark 9:33-34.)

Questions on

Mark

Chapter 10

Mark 10:1-12 Divorce

441. What was the 'test' in asking the Lord "Is it lawful for a man to divorce his wife?"

442. What does the Law of Moses say about divorce? (See Deuteronomy 24:1-4.)

443. Under what circumstances did the Law of Moses permit divorce?

444. During the New Testament times, under what circumstances did the Pharisees (a) allow a man to divorce his wife; (b) allow a wife to divorce her husband?

445. If God's ideal is that a husband and wife should not separate, why did He permit divorce?

446. If God's ideal is that a husband and wife should not separate, is divorce a 'sin'?

447. If a man divorces his wife and marries another woman, he commits adultery against his first wife. Does that mean his first wife is free to remarry? (See Matthew 5:31-32; 19:1-9.)

448. If she did not remarry, what would she do to make ends meet?

449. If a woman divorces her husband and marries another man, she commits adultery against her first husband. Does that mean her first husband is free to remarry? (See Matthew 5:31-32; 19:1-19.)

450. How does the teaching of Luke 16:18 fit in with the teaching on divorce in Deuteronomy, Matthew and Mark?

Mark 10:13-16 Jesus and the Little Children

451. Why did the people want Jesus to 'touch' the little children?

452. Why did the disciples rebuke the parents?

453. What was the Lord's reaction to the disciples?

454. What does the Lord mean by the expression "such as these"?

455. In what ways must an adult be 'like a little child'?

456. What did the Lord do or say when he 'blessed' the children?

Mark 10:17-31 The Rich Young Man

457. Why did the man call Jesus 'good'?

458. Did calling someone 'good' imply you thought that he was the Messiah?

459. If eternal life is a gift from God to those who have faith in Him, why did the man ask what he had to 'do' to inherit eternal life?

460. What did the Lord Jesus tell him he had to 'do'?

461. Had the man done all these?

462. Were they sufficient to gain him eternal life?

463. What additional thing had the man to do? Why did he have to do this?

464. Did he do this additional thing?

465. Would we do what the Lord Jesus commanded the young man to do?

466. Is it easy or hard or impossible for the rich to enter the kingdom of God by what they 'do'?

467. Is it easy or hard or impossible for anyone to enter the kingdom of God by what they 'do'?

468. If people find it impossible to 'do' what God wants them to 'do' to inherit eternal life, what is God's solution? How does He make it possible for people to be saved and inherit eternal life? (See problem passage 31 of Michael Penny's *40 Problem Passages* for additional information on Mark 10:23-25 in the light of Galatians 5:21.)

469. What did the Lord promise 'in this present age' to those who had given up things for Him?

470. Did this happen to, for example, the disciples?

471. Is it truth for this dispensation of grace in which we live?

472. What would they receive in 'the age to come'?

473. To whom was the Lord referring when he said, "The first will be last, and the last first"? In His day, who were the 'first'? Who were the 'last'?

Mark 10:32-34 Jesus predicts His death and resurrection

474. Why were the disciples 'astonished'? What were they astonished by?

475. Why were the rest of the followers 'afraid'? What were they afraid of?

476. What two things were the chief priests and the teachers of the law going to do to the Lord?

477. What four things were the Gentiles going to do to the Lord?

478. What was to happen three days later?

Mark 10:35-45 The request of James and John

479. What was the significance of sitting one on Christ's right hand and the other on His left?

480. What did James and John mean by 'in your glory'?

481. Why did the Lord say to them, "You do not know what you are asking"?

482. To what is Jesus referring when He asked them "Can you drink the cup I drink?"

483. To what is Jesus referring when He asked them "Can you be baptized with the baptism I am baptized with"?

484. What was James' and John's answer?

485. How did James and John drink of the cup and how were they baptized? (For James' martyrdom see Acts 12:1-2 and for John's see Josephus *The Antiquities of the Jews* 20,9,1 and Appendix 2 of *Approaching the Bible* by Michael Penny.)

486. Who will sit at Christ's left and right hand?

487. Why were the ten indignant with James and John?

488. What was the relevancy of the leaders of the Gentiles? Why did the Lord talk about them and what they did?

489. How were the disciples, as leaders, to behave?

490. Who was the perfect role model they were to emulate?

491. If what ways did this model fulfill His role?

Mark 10:46-52 Blind Bartimaeus

492. Why did Bartimaeus shout?

493. Why did some people rebuke Bartimaeus and tell him to stop shouting?

494. Why did Bartimaues think Jesus could heal him?

495. The *NIV* has "You faith has *healed* you." The *KJV* has "thy faith has *made thee whole*", but with a margin note giving an alternative "thy faith has *saved* thee". Which is correct? (For a discussion on the Greek word *sozo*, to be saved, in passages such as this see pages 107 to 115 of *The Miracles of the Apostles* by Michael Penny.)

Questions on Mark Chapter 11

Mark 11:1-11 The Triumphal Entry

496. To which village did the Lord send two of His disciples?
497. What is a colt?
498. What is significant about the colt not having been ridden?
499. Why did they their cloaks over the colt?
500. Would it be normal for a colt, which had never been ridden, to let someone sit on its back and ride it?
501. Why did the Lord want to ride a colt? (Cp. Matthew 21:4-5.)
502. Why did the people spread their cloaks on the ground?
503. Why did others cut branches from the fields and spread them on the ground?
504. John 12:13 tells us they took "Palm branches". Is there any significance in them being 'palm' branches?
505. What does *hosanna* mean?
506. Why did the people shout *hosanna*?
507. Who did the people think the Lord was when they shouted, "Blessed is *he* who comes in the name of the Lord"?
508. What is the "*kingdom* of our father David" to which the people referred?
509. How far is it from Jerusalem to Bethany?

Mark 11:12-14 The Fig Tree

510. Why didn't Jesus have something to eat before they left Bethany?
511. Why did the Lord 'curse' the fig tree if it was "not the season for figs"?
512. Is there some sort of significance or symbolism for Israel in the fig tree episode?

Mark 11:14-19 Jesus Clears the Temple

513. As many Jews of the dispersion came to Jerusalem to offer sacrifices to God, what was wrong with people selling such things as lambs and doves to them for their sacrifices?

514. As these Jews of the dispersion came from many different countries (see Acts 2:5-11, for example) what would be wrong in having money changers to help them change their money into the local currency?

515. Why did the Lord calls these merchants and money changes 'robbers'?

516. What sort of merchandise was not allowed to be carried through the temple courts?

517. For what two reasons did the chief priests and teachers of the Law want to kill Jesus?

518. In the evening, when they left, where did they go to?

Mark 11:20-21 The Withered Fig Tree

519. Is there any significance in the fact that the fig tree withered "from its roots"?

520. Is that the normal way a plant, bush or tree withers?

521. If not, how could it wither from the root up?

Mark 11:22-23 Faith

522. Which mountain is the Lord referring to when He says, "*This mountain*"?

523. In verse 23, is the Lord talking literally, using a figure of speech (and if so, which one), or hypothetically?

524. Are they any examples in the rest of the New Testament, or in the Old Testament, where physical objects (e.g. a mountain, a tree, see Luke 17:6, or anything else) were moved by faith?

525. If not, does that mean that no one had sufficient faith, not even the size of a mustard seed (Luke 17:6), or that the Lord was speaking figuratively or hypothetically?

Mark 11:24 Prayer

526. Did the disciples get everything they asked for in the Acts and their Epistles?

527. If not was if because they did not believe?

528. Do such words as "whatever", "everything", and "everyone" always take on their *literal* meaning? Or do they most often have a *limited* meaning? (For a fuller discussion on the issues raised by the subjects in this verse see problem passages 7,8 and 20 in Michael Penny's *40 Problem Passages*.)

529. In verse 24 we read, "it *will* be yours." Why do the Gospels and the writings of Peter, James, and John use "will" in association with prayer, yet the Apostle Paul us "may" in his writings? (See *Unanswered Prayer* by Neville Stephens.)

Mark 11:25 Forgiveness

530. Was it true, at that time, that the Jews had to forgive others in order to be forgiven by God?

531. If so, (a) what was the point of the sin offering, and (b) how could Abraham's faith be counted as righteousness, ensuring him forgiveness?

532. What about us today? Do we need to forgive to be forgiven? (See Ephesians 4:32 & Colossians 3:13.)

533. Is there another *type* of forgiveness, other than the forgiveness of sins for eternal life, which have by grace through faith in Christ dying for our sins?

534. Or is there another *purpose* or *reason* for forgiveness? (See problem passages 21 and 35 in *40 Problem Passages* by Michael Penny.)

Mark 11:27-33 The Authority of Jesus Questioned

535. What was the point, or purpose, behind the two questions which the chief priests, teachers and elders asked the Lord?
536. What did the Lord mean by John's baptism being "from *heaven*"?
537. What did He mean by John's baptism being "from *men*"?
538. Why did the Lord's question put the leaders in a quandary?

Questions on Mark Chapter 12

Mark 12:1-12 The Parable of the Tenants

539. To whom did the Lord tell this parable?

540. Why did the man in the parable put a wall around the vineyard?

541. Why did he build a watchtower?

542. For what reasons did the farmers treat the servants so badly?

543. Why did the farmers decide to kill the owner's only son?

544. Why did the Lord quote Psalm 118:22-23?

545. What was said in this parable to make them realise the Lord was speaking against them? Who, in the parable, represented them?

546. Why did they not arrest Him then and there?

Mark 12:13-17 Paying Taxes to Caesar

547. Who were the Herodians? What did they believe?

548. Who were the Pharisees? What did they believe?

549. What did the Herodians and Pharisees have in common?

550. Why did they want to catch out the Lord?

551. What did they hope to achieve by their question?

552. Why were they amazed at the Lord's answer?

Mark 12:18-27 Marriage and the Resurrection

553. Who were the Sadducees? What did they believe?

554. Why did they ask him a question about resurrection?

555. Which part of the Law of Moses did they refer to?

556. Did they quote it exactly and correctly?

557. Jesus said they "did not know the Scriptures". Which Scriptures did they not know?

558. Why did they not know or understand the power of God?

559. When the dead rise will they be "angels in heaven" or be "*like* angels in heaven"? If the latter, in which way will the raised be *like* angels? In which ways will they *not* be like angels?

560. How does the quotation from Deuteronomy 6:4-5 prove that people will be resurrected from the dead?

561. How bad a mistake is it not to believe in the resurrection of people?

Mark 12:28-34 The Greatest Commandment

562. What were the motives and reasons for the question asked by the Pharisees and Herodians? (vs 13-15)

563. What were the motives and reasons for the question asked by the Sadducees? (vs 18-23)

564. What were the motives and reasons for the question asked by the Teacher of the Law? (v 28)

565. Is it right or wrong to question?

566. Why did the Lord give two commandments in His answer and not just one, as He had been asked?

567. Which were the two commandments that Jesus cited?

568. Why did He choose these two?

569. What reason did the Teacher of the Law give for agreeing with Jesus?

570. What did the Lord say to this teacher?

571. Why did no one ask him any more questions from then on? (Consider the wider context:
e.g. from 11:27 to 12:34.)

Mark 12:35-40 Whose Son is the Christ?

572. Were the Teachers of the Law wrong to say that the Christ (Messiah) was to be the Son of David? (i.e. come through David's line of descendants.)

573. What did it mean when David called the Messiah "Lord"?
574. How can the Messiah be both David's Lord and David's Son?
575. Why were the large crowd delighted by these questions from the Lord Jesus? Was it because they understood the theological arguments or was it because the Teachers of the Law could not answer and were shown up?
576. What four things did the Teachers of the Law like to do?
577. What two other things did they do?
578. Why did they like to walk around in flowing robes?
579. What does it mean to "devour widows' houses"? Why did they do this?
580. What were, or will be, the severe punishments such men will receive?

Mark 12:41-44 The Widow's Offering

581. What was the temple treasury?
582. Which of the offerings from the Mosaic Law were put into it?
583. How much were the rich people putting in?
584. How much did the poor widow put in?
585. Why, in the Lord's eyes, had she put in more?
586. Do we give out of our wealth or out of our poverty?

Questions on Mark Chapter 13

Mark 13:1-4 The Temple

587. What was in the disciples' minds when they looked at the temple?

588. Were the disciples more impressed with the temple than they were with the Lord Jesus Christ?

589. What was the effect upon the disciples of what the Lord said to them?

590. How long did they think about it, and possibly talk about it? (That is, how long did it take to walk from the temple to the Mount of Olives?)

591. What *two* questions did the disciples ask Him?

592. Did the Lord Jesus give precise answers to both of the questions, one of them, or neither of them? (See verses 5-27.)

593. To which question did He give the fullest answer? (See verses 5-27.)

Mark 13:5-8 The Beginning of Birth Pains

594. What was the first thing the Lord Jesus told them to look out for?

595. What form is the deception to take?

596. Did this happen during the Acts period, or up to AD 70, the year that temple was destroyed?

597. Has it happened at anytime in the past? If so, when, and will it happen again in the future? If it has not happened in the past, when will it happen?

598. What was the second thing the Lord Jesus told them to look out for?

599. When these things happened, did they signal the end?

600. Did these things happen during the Acts period, or up to AD 70?

601. Have they happened anytime in the past? If so, when, and will they happen again in the future? If they have not happened in the past, when will they happen?

602. To which nations and kingdoms is the Lord Jesus Christ referring?

603. What other two things are to happen?

604. Where are they to happen?

605. Did they happen during the Acts period, or up to AD 70?

606. Have they happened anytime in the past? If so, when, and will they happen again in the future? If they have not happened in the past, when will they happen?

607. What did the Lord Jesus mean by describing the time when all these events happen as "the beginning of birth pains"?

Mark 13:9-13 Be on your guard

608. Why must the disciples be on their guard?

609. What three things are to happen to them?

610. Did these happen to them during the Acts period, or up to AD 70??

611. What must happen first; i.e. *before* the temple is destroyed (verses 3-4)?

612. When arrested and brought to trial, why did the disciples have no need to worry?

613. Did this happen during the Acts period, or up to AD 70?

614. What is to happen to family relationships?

615. Did this happen during the Acts period, or up to AD 70?

616. Why were people to hate the disciples?

617. What is the 'end' to which the Lord Jesus is referring in verse 13?

618. What does He mean by 'saved' in that verse? (He cannot be referring to salvation from sin.)

Mark 13:14-20 Unequalled Distress

619. What is the "abomination that causes desolation"? (See Daniel 9:27; 11:31; 12:11)

620. Where is it to stand? (Compare Matthew 24:15. See also Michael Penny's *The Mark of the Beast and the Jerusalem Temple*, available from the Open Bible Trust at $1.25.)

621. Which people are to "flee to the mountains"?

622. Did all this happen during the Acts period, or up to AD 70?

623. Has it happened at anytime since? If so, when? If not, when will it happen?

624. Why should people on the roof of the house, not enter their house?

625. Why should people in the field, go back home for their cloak?

626. Why will it be dreadful for pregnant women and nursing mothers?

627. Why should they pray that these events will not take place in winter?

628. If the Lord did not step in and stop these days, what would happen?

629. Why does the Lord decide to step in and curtail this time?

630. Who are the elect? (Don't forget verse 14.)

631. Has all this happened in the past, or is it to happen in the future?

Mark 13:21-27 At that time

632. At that time, what are some people likely to say?

633. What sort of people are to appear?

634. What will these people do?

635. At that time, what is to happen to the sun?

636. What will happen to the moon?

637. What is to happen to the stars?

638. Is this literal, or figurative? If figurative, what does the figure mean?

639. What is to happen to the heavenly bodies?

640. Is this literal or figurative? If figurative, what does the figure mean?

641. Has all of this happened in the past, or is it still future?

642. At that time, after all this, what are men to see?

643. Is this 'all' men in the world, or those in Judea (verse 14)?

644. What is the first thing the Lord is to do?

645. Who are the elect? (Compare verse 20 and note verse 14.)

Mark 13:28-31 The fig tree

646. When the twigs on a fig tree get tender and the leaves come out, could they tell precisely how long it was before summer?

647. When people see "these things" happening, what will they know?

648. What does the Lord mean by "these things"? Everything from verse 5 to verse 24? Or just those in verses 14-19? Or some other selection?

649. What is the "it" to which Christ refers in verse 29?

650. The words of verse 30, "this generation will certainly not pass away until all these things have happened" are a problem in the English. There are three explanations:

(a) The *NIV* footnote has 'race' for 'generation'; implying that the Jewish race will not pass away before the Lord returns.

(b) Another suggestion is that the verse should read "that" generation, referring to some future generation of Jews living in Judea. In other words, all the events will happen within a span of 40 years

(c) *The Companion Bible* states that the word "until" (*eos an*, in the Greek) is conditional, and that Christ was teaching that all these things *could* have happened within the lifetime of that generation if ... the "if" being the Jews' acceptance of Jesus as their Messiah either when He was on earth, or during the period of time covered by the Acts of the Apostles (see Acts 3:19-21).

Discuss these three explanations, bearing in mind Christ's strong affirmation of what He said in verse 31.

Mark 13:32-37 The Day and the Hour

651. Which "day or hour" is the Lord referring to?

652. Although no-one can work out the "day or hour", will those alive near that time be able to work out the year? Or even the month?

653. Why will the people need to be alert? What will they need to guard against?

654. When a man goes away, do his servants have some idea when he will return?

655. Do the servants know the "day or hour" he is to return?

656. Why does the Lord tell the disciples to "Watch!"?

657. What is it they are to watch for?

Questions on Mark Chapter 14

Mark 14:1-11 The Lord is Anointed at Bethany

658. What is the difference between 'The Passover' and 'The Feast of Unleavened Bread'?

659. Why didn't the leaders want to arrest Jesus during the Feast of Unleavened Bread? Was it a real worry?

660. What is an 'alabaster' box?

661. What is 'nard'?

662. Why did she 'break' the box?

663. Why did the people in Simon the Leper's house rebuke the woman harshly? If Simon the Leper was not able to work, were not their comments understandable?

664. Did the Lord rebuke the people in Simon's house gently or harshly?

665. Why were the chief priests delighted to see Judas? (Cp. verses 1-2.)

Mark 14:12-26 The Lord's Supper

666. What was the link between 'The Passover' and 'The Feast of Unleavened Bread'?

667. Where would they have sacrificed the Passover lamb?

668. Did they eat the Passover lamb after it had been sacrificed?

669. Why did they need to make 'preparations' for the Passover? What needed to be done?

670. Had the Lord Jesus made arrangements with the man carrying the water jar before hand, or was this an example of His divine foreknowledge?

671. Had the Lord Jesus made arrangements beforehand with the owner of the house?

672. Was the Passover a time of celebration?

673. At the Passover, would the normal mood have been congenial and happy?

674. What change of mood would have taken place when the Lord told them that one of them was going to betray Him? Did they believe Him?

675. The Lord Jesus refers to a 'covenant': what is a covenant?

676. To which covenant was the Lord referring? (See Jeremiah 31:31-34.)

677. With whom did God make this covenant?

678. Has the kingdom of God come in? If so, when did the Lord drink again 'the fruit of the vine'?

Mark 14:27-31 The Lord Predicts Peter's Denials

679. The Lord Jesus told them that 'all' would fall away: when did John fall away?

680. Did He make it clear to them that He was to rise from the dead?

681. Why was Peter so emphatic that he would never deny Christ?

682. Did the others also deny that they would deny Christ? Did Judas, or had he left?

Mark 14:43-52 The Garden of Gethsemane

683. Why did the Lord leave some of His disciples at one place, but take Peter, James and John with Him?

684. Why was Christ at 'the point of death', then and there, in the garden?

685. Was Christ asking for the cup of death, which was close to Him then and there in the garden, to be taken away? Or was He asking for death on the Cross to be taken away? (Cp. John 18:11.)

686. If Christ had died in the garden, could that have been counted as a sacrifice for the sins of the world?

687. Why were the disciples so tired?

Mark 14:43-52 The Lord is arrested

688. Were there any Roman soldiers in the crowd that came to arrest the Lord?

689. Why did Judas use a 'kiss' as the signal to the men who came to arrest the Lord?

690. Did all of the disciples desert Him at that time?

691. Did Peter and John return later to be closer to Jesus?

692. Who was the young man wearing a linen garment?

Mark 14: 53-65 Before theSanhedrin

693. Before whom did Jesus appear?

694. What were they looking for?

695. How many testified against the Lord?

696. Why could their testimony not be used?

697. Why did the Lord Jesus not answer their accusations?

698. What specific question did the high priest ask Jesus?

699. What was the Lord's two word answer, and how did expand and emphasis this?

700. Why did the high priest state that they had heard 'blasphemy'? What is 'blasphemy'?

701. Why did the high priest tear his clothes?

702. Why were they wrong to condemn Christ? If anyone else had given that answer to that question, they would have been right!

703. Why did they blindfold Him, strike Him, and then ask Him to prophesy?

704. Where was Peter while all this was going on?

Mark 14:66-72 Peter disowns the Lord

705. Who spoke to Peter first? What did she say?

706. What was Peter's answer, and what did he do?

707. Who spoke of Peter next? To whom did she speak? And what did she say?

708. What was Peter's reaction?

709. Who spoke to Peter next? How did they know that Peter was a Galilean?

710. What was Peter's reaction to their challenge?

711. What was Peter's reaction when he heard the rooster crow?

Questions on Mark Chapter 15

Mark 15:1-15 Jesus before Pilate

712. Who were the people who reached a decision about the Lord Jesus? How many of them were there?

713. What was the decision they reached? (See Mark 14:63-65.)

714. What is the connection between "the Christ ... the Son of the Blessed One" (Mark 14:61), and "the king of the Jews" (Mark 15:2)? (Compare Matthew 2:2 and 2:4.)

715. What specific things did the chief priests accuse Jesus of before Pilate?

716. Why did the Lord's refusal to answer these accusations "amaze" Pilate?

717. Why had the chief priests handed the Lord over to Pilate?

718. Who was Barabas and why was he in prison?

719. When the crowd were asked what crime Jesus had committed, what was their answer?

720. Why was the crowd so hostile towards the Lord when, the previous week, they had shouted "Hosanna! Blessed is he who comes in the name of the Lord"? What changed them? (See Mark 11:1-11.)

721. If Pilate was going to crucify Christ, why did he have Him flogged first? What was the point?

Mark 15:16-20 The Soldiers mock the Lord

722. Why did the soldiers put a "purple" robe on Jesus?

723. Why did the soldiers strike Him on the head with a staff?

724. Why did they spit on Him?

725. Why did they fall on their knees and pay homage to Him?

726. What was the Lord's reaction to all of this?

Mark 15:21-32 The Crucifixion

727. Why was Simon of Cyrene forced to carry the cross for the Lord?

728. Why did the people offer Jesus wine mixed with myrrh?

729. Why did He refuse that drink?

730. Why did they cast lots for His clothes?

731. About what time of day was "the third hour"?

732. What insults were hurled at Him while He hung on the cross?

733. Could Jesus have come down from the cross if He had wanted to?

734. If He had come down off the cross, would the chief priests and teachers have believed in Him?

Mark 15:33-41 The Death of Jesus

735. What times were "the sixth hour" and "the ninth hour"?

736. Why did Jesus cry out, "My God! My God! Why have you forsaken me"? What had happened?

737. Why did some think He was calling to Elijah?

738. Why did they think that Elijah might come and take Him down?

739. Why did they offer Him vinegar to drink?

740. Why was the curtain temple torn from top to bottom? How did it happen? What did it signify? (See number 13 of *40 Problem Passages* by Michael Penny.)

741. What was it that impressed the centurion and made him say "Surely this man was the Son of God!"?

742. Who was there, at the cross, when the Lord Jesus breathed His last?

Mark 15:42-47 The Burial of Jesus

743. What was the purpose of the "Preparation Day"? What was it to 'prepare' for?

744. Did Joseph of Arimathea believe that Jesus was the Christ, the Son of God?

745. Why did he want the body of Jesus?

746. What surprised Pilate?

747. What did Joseph do with then Lord's body? Why did he do this?

748. Was Joseph known to Mary Magdalene and the other Mary?

Questions on Mark Chapter 16

Mark 16:1-8 The Resurrection

749 . When would the Sabbath be over?

750 . Which day was 'the first day of the week'?

751 . What problem did the women anticipate?

752 . Who was the young man sitting inside the tomb?

753 . What did the young man say to them?

754 . What affect did his words have on them?

755 . Did they believe what he said?

756 . Why didn't they follow his instructions and tell Peter and the disciples?

Mark 16:9-14 The Appearances

757. To whom did Jesus appear first?

758. Who did she tell about His resurrection?

759. Why didn't they believe her?

760. To whom did the Lord appear next?

761. Who did they tell about His resurrection?

762. Why weren't their testimony believed?

763. What convinced the Eleven that Jesus had risen from the dead?

764. What did Christ say to the Eleven?

Mark 16:15-19 Final Instruction

765.   Where did the Lord tell them to go?

766.   What were they to preach?

767.   What were they to do?

768.   What five things were to accompany those who believed?

769.   Why was it necessary for the Eleven to have these miraculous signs?

770.   Where did the Lord go after He had finished talking to them?

771.   What did the disciples do after the Lord had left them?

Having completed this study of Mark's Gospel, it would be a good idea to read right through Mark's Gospel again. This will be of great help and the reader may be surprised how much is recalled and how much has been learnt.

Also, having gone through Mark's Gospel, you may care to consider the piece of writing which cover the next historical events, and you may care to use the following study guide:

Search The Acts of the Apostles

A Study Guide to
the Fifth Book of the New Testament

By Michael Penny and Neville Stephens

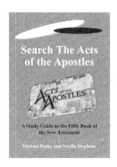

Other Study Guides

A Study Guide to Psalm 119
By Michael Penny

A very useful guide to Psalm 119 indicating ...

- It is the longest Psalm;

- It is an Acrostic Psalm – and gives an acrostic translation of the first 24 verses;

- The Ten Hebrews words which recur throughout the Psalm.

Each group of eight verses is considered separately – giving 22 studies.

Each group is given in two translation presented in parallel for ease of comparison.

For each group a task is set for personals study or group discussion.

And at the end of each group, as a conclusion, there is page or so of commentary.

Manual on the Gospel of John

By Michael Penny

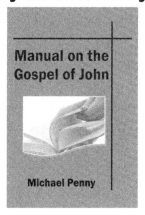

This book was produced with college students for college students, but is valuable for any age range. It asks and answers the questions the students aske about John's Gospel, but in a novel way.

The book is in four parts:

1) Aims of the Book; How to use the Book
2) Questions with Aids and Hints to the Answers
3) Questions with Answers and Further Information
4) Main themes of John's Gospel

This book is ideal for not only for personal study, but also for Youth Groups, House Groups, and Bible Study Groups. The questions in Section Two can be discussed and answered, and there and Aids and Hints to help. After being discussed and answered, the author's answers and comments can be reviewed from Section Three.

"If you are stuck for an idea with your group, try The Manual on the Gospel of John." (Eric Thorn, reviewed in *The Connexion)*

Further details of all the books mentioned on these pages can be seen on

www.obt.org.uk

They can also be ordered from that website and also from:

The Open Bible Trust,
Fordland Mount, Upper Basildon,
Reading, RG8 8LU, UK.

They are also available as eBooks from Amazon and Apple and as KDP paperbacks from Amazon.

 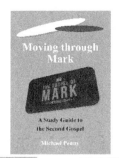 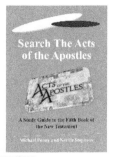

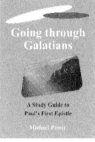 

Learning from Luke

A Study Guide to the Gospel sent to a Gentile

Moving through Mark

A Study Guide to the Second Gospel

Search the Acts of the Apostles

A Study Guide to the
Fifth Book of the New Testament

Going through Galatians

A Study Guide to Paul's First Letter

About the author

Michael Penny was born in Ebbw Vale, Gwent, Wales in 1943. He read Mathematics at the University of Reading, before teaching for twelve years and becoming the Director of Mathematics and Business Studies at Queen Mary's College Basingstoke in Hampshire, England. In 1978 he entered Christian publishing, and in 1984 became the administrator of The Open Bible Trust.

He held this position for seven years, before moving to the USA and becoming pastor of Grace Church in New Berlin, Wisconsin. He returned to Britain in 1999, and is at present the Administrator and Editor of The Open Bible Trust. From 2010 he has been Chairman of Churches Together in Reading, where he speaks in a number of churches of different denominations. He is also a member of the Advisory Committee to Reading University Christian Union and a chaplain at Reading College.

He is lead chaplain for Activate Learning and has set up chaplaincy teams in a number of their colleges including Reading College, The City of Oxford College, Bracknell and Wokingham College, and Blackbird Leys College.

He lives near Reading with his wife and has appeared on Premier Radio and BBC Radio Berkshire many times. He has made several speaking tours of America, Canada, Australia, New Zealand and the Netherlands, as well as others to South Africa and the Philippines. Some of his writings have been translated into German and Russian.

Also by Michael Penny

He has written many books including:

40 Problem Passages,
Galatians: Interpretation and Application,
Joel's Prophecy: Past and Future,
Approaching the Bible,
The Miracles of the Apostles,
The Manual on the Gospel of John
The Bible! Myth or Message?

Plus two written with W M Henry:

The Will of God: Past and Present
Following Philippians
Abraham and his seed (with chapters by Sylvia Penny also)

His latest three books are:

James: His life and letter
Peter: His life and letters.
Paul: A Missionary of Genius

Further details of all these books can be seen on

www.obt.org.uk

from where they can also be ordered.

They are also available as eBooks from Amazon and Apple and as KDP paperbacks from Amazon.

Further details of the books on these pages
can be seen on

www.obt.org.uk

The books are available from that website and from

The Open Bible Trust
Fordland Mount, Upper Basildon,
Reading, RG8 8LU, UK.

They are also available as eBooks from Amazon and
Apple and as
KDP paperback from Amazon

Further reading

The Miracles of the Apostles
Michael Penny

Why did the Apostles perform miracles?
Why were they able to perform them?
What was the purpose of the miracles?
What did they signify to the Jews?
Why did the Gentiles misunderstand them?
Why was Paul, later, not able to heal?
When did the miracles cease?
Why did they cease?

This book answers these questions, explains the significance and purpose of each type of miracle performed by the Apostles, and makes it clear why such miracles are not in evidence today.

Salvation

Safe and Secure
Sylvia Penny

This important book is a thorough treatment of the subject of salvation, asking such questions as ...

- **What is it, exactly, that saves us?**
- **Is salvation secure?**
- **Can it be lost?**
- **What is 'conditional security'?**

It deals with a wide number of issues such as ...

- **Salvation and works**
- **The doctrine of rewards**
- **Lordship salvation**
- **Free grace theology**
- **Assurance of salvation**
- **Why people lose their faith**

Search magazine

Michael Penny is editor of *Search* magazine.

For a free sample of
The Open Bible Trust's magazine *Search*,
please email

admin@obt.org.uk

or visit

www.obt.org.uk/search

About this Book

Moving through Mark
A Study Guide to the
Second Gospel

This book takes people through the Mark's Gospel with a series of guided questions. In all there are over 780 questions: that is 45 to 50 on each chapter.

These questions first appeared in a series published in *Search* magazine some time ago, and they were so well received that it has been decided to publish them so that other may benefit from them.

Individual readers can ponder these questions, meditate upon them, and consider an answer.

These question can also stimulate groups to deliberate upon them and discuss them, and so come to a joint response with respect to the answers.

This is an ideal study guide to the second Gospel as these questions bring out a wealth of information and teaching.

Publications of The Open Bible Trust must be in accordance with its evangelical, fundamental and dispensational basis. However, beyond this minimum, writers are free to express whatever beliefs they may have as their own understanding, provided that the aim in so doing is to further the object of The Open Bible Trust. A copy of the doctrinal basis is available on **www.obt.org.uk** or from:

THE OPEN BIBLE TRUST
Fordland Mount, Upper Basildon,
Reading, RG8 8LU, UK

Printed in Great Britain
by Amazon